LOW FAT

hamlyn

kitchen library

LOW FAT

Sally Mansfield

First published in the U.K. in 1998
by Hamlyn, a division of
Octopus Publishing Group Limited
2–4 Heron Quays, London E14 4JP

This edition first published in 2001

ISBN 0 600 60478 0

Printed in China

NOTES

Both metric and imperial measurements have been given in all
recipes. Use one set of measurements only and not a
mixture of both.

Standard level spoon measurements are used in all recipes.
1 tablespoon = one 15 ml spoon
1 teaspoon = one 5 ml spoon

Eggs should be medium to large unless otherwise stated.
The Department of Health advises that eggs should not be
consumed raw. This book contains dishes made with raw or
lightly cooked eggs. It is prudent for more vulnerable people such
as pregnant and nursing mothers, invalids, the elderly, babies and
young children to avoid uncooked or lightly cooked dishes made
with eggs. Once prepared, these dishes should be kept
refrigerated and used promptly.

Meat and poultry should be cooked thoroughly. To test if poultry
is cooked, pierce the flesh through the thickest part with a
skewer or fork – the juices should run clear, never pink or red.

Do not re-freeze a dish that has been frozen previously.

Pepper should be freshly ground black pepper unless
otherwise stated.

Fresh herbs should be used, unless otherwise stated. If
unavailable, use dried herbs as an alternative but halve the
quantities stated.

Measurements for canned food have been given as a standard
metric equivalent.

Nuts and nut derivatives
This book includes dishes made with nuts and nut derivatives. It
is advisable for customers with known allergic reactions to nuts
and nut derivatives and those who may be potentially vulnerable
to these allergies, such as pregnant and nursing mothers,
invalids, the elderly, babies and children, to avoid dishes made
with nuts and nut oils. It is also prudent to check the labels of
pre-prepared ingredients for the possible inclusion of nut
derivatives.

Ovens should be preheated to the specified temperature – if
using a fan-assisted oven, follow the manufacturer's
instructions for adjusting the time and the temperature.

All the recipes in this book have been analysed by a profes-
sional nutritionist, so that you can see their nutritional content
at a glance. The abbreviations are as follows: Kcal = calories;
KJ = kilojoules; CHO = carbohydrate. The analysis refers to each
serving, unless otherwise stated, and does not include optional
ingredients.

Contents

Introduction

Compared with 20 years ago, the foods we eat and how we cook them have changed beyond recognition. With the availability of ingredients flown in from all over the globe, and people now travelling more than ever and encountering cuisines from different regions, it is hardly surprising that our diets have changed greatly, too.

We have also become much more aware of what we should and should not eat. Many of us crave creamy sauces or slices of wicked chocolate gâteau and, occasionally, why not tuck in and have a treat? On a daily basis, however, it is wiser to keep clear of highly fatty foods and increase our intake of foods high in protein and carbohydrates instead. As this book shows, this does not necessarily mean missing out on flavour, it just means adopting a slightly different approach to choosing and using ingredients.

MAKING THE MOST OF INGREDIENTS

Fat adds moisture to foods, so when cooking without it you need to ensure food doesn't dry out, either by covering it with foil or by basting with water or stock, so that the food almost steams and the natural flavours come through. Fresh spices and herbs can be used to add flavour to meats, fish and vegetables, so that you don't notice the lack of fat. Delicate foods such as fish cook well with simple fresh herbs such as parsley and also work well with sharp citrus flavours. An alternative to fat in cooking is low-fat yogurt. A little yogurt, combined with a spicy paste, for example, is useful for not only adding moisture, but balancing the final flavour, too.

FOODS TO AVOID

One of the easiest ways to control your intake of fat is by avoiding most processed foods, such as crisps and snacks, biscuits, cakes, ice creams, sauces such as mayonnaise and even some types of bread. They not only contain a high proportion of fat, but it is usually difficult to work out exactly how much they do contain, making monitoring your fat intake rather difficult. It is therefore a good idea to make you own, if possible. Contrary to popular belief, making your own bread is simple and you can control what goes into it. You also get the benefit of delicious home-baked bread into the bargain. Try one of the bread recipes in the first section and you will soon be making your own bread on a regular basis.

Kneading Bread Dough

All yeast doughs must be kneaded to strengthen the dough and help it to rise. After mixing the ingredients, gather the dough into a ball and turn it out onto a well-floured surface. Flatten it slightly, hold down the front of the dough with one hand and stretch out the far side with the other. Lift the far side and fold it over towards you.

Press down firmly, then use the heel of your hand to push the dough away from you with a punching movement. Give the dough a quarter turn and repeat the stretching, folding, punching and turning movements for about 10 minutes, until the dough is firm, elastic and smooth. Place the dough in an oiled bowl, cover with a clean, damp tea towel and leave to rise in a warm place for about 1 hour or until the dough has doubled in size.

Knock back the risen dough by turning it onto a floured surface and kneading it with your knuckles. This knocks out the air bubbles created by the yeast, leading to a more even texture.

The dough can then be shaped according to the recipe or placed in a loaf tin, and left to rise again in a warm place for about 1 hour, before baking.

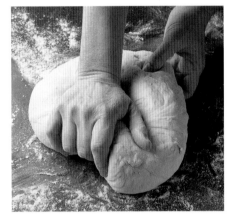

LOW-FAT FOODS

Naturally low-fat foods are the truly good guys to put in the shopping basket. The main ones are vegetables, some of which, like potatoes, are high in carbohydrates and therefore great energy givers, too. And don't forget leafy and root vegetables. They are not only delicious, but also high in vitamins, minerals and fibre. White fish is also a low-fat food and you will find many recipes using a variety of white and oily fish in the fish chapter. In addition, fish cooks very quickly, which helps to maintain its natural vitamins and minerals. Grains, such as rice, and pulses are also naturally low in fat.

The dairy cabinets in the shops are bursting with low-fat alternatives these days and many of them can be easily substituted for their high-fat equivalents. Always check the nutritional advice on the pack and work out the fat grams per 25 g/1 oz for an accurate idea of how much you can use. Although low-fat yogurt tastes a little sharp, by the time you have stirred in a little honey or fresh fruit, the flavour is delicious.

STORECUPBOARD SAVERS

If you really want to maintain a low-fat diet, then you will need to give the store cupboard a face lift. Check the items you have in there and if they are high in fat, use them up or throw them away and then start stocking the cupboard with lower fat varieties. Canned foods will be generally low in fat, but when buying canned meats and fish, make sure you choose wisely. Tuna in brine or water tastes just as good as tuna packed in oil, for example. Also take care with ready-prepared sauces. Mayonnaise and salad cream have large amounts of fat.

Condiments and flavourings, such as Worcestershire sauce and vinegars make a huge difference to bland foods; a dash here and there will pep things up greatly. Salads usually need a dressing; you can buy some low-fat convenience products, but a splash of balsamic vinegar will make the perfect low-fat finish to a bowl of leaves.

For an alternative when frying, try an oil in spray form as it is easier to use far less of this than oil from a bottle. Look out for extra virgin olive oil spray – just a few light sprays will coat the pan you want to cook in and stop the food from sticking, and at a fraction of the fat intake.

COOKING THE LOW-FAT WAY

When embarking on a new style of cooking, which will hopefully lead to an entirely new way of eating, invest in a few good-quality nonstick pans. Stainless steel pans tend to stick unless well oiled and for true low-fat cooking you don't want to be adding too much, if any, fat to the pan.

A nonstick wok is recommended. It creates a hot base for whatever you want to stir-fry and cooks food very quickly, keeping in as many of the vitamins and minerals as possible.

The trick to creating truly tasty meals without the fat is in the combination of ingredients used. The recipes in this book will not only make your mouth water but also satisfy everyone at the table.

BASIC RECIPES

Homemade stock is twice as delicious as shop-bought alternatives, and by making your own, you can monitor your fat intake more accurately. The following recipes are for stocks that are low in fat, but very high in flavour.

VEGETABLE STOCK

3 potatoes, peeled and chopped
1 onion, thinly sliced
2 leeks, chopped
2 celery sticks, chopped
2 carrots, peeled and chopped
1 small fennel head, thinly sliced
2 bay leaves
few thyme sprigs
few parsley stalks
salt and pepper

1 Put the vegetables into a large pan with the herbs and add 1.5 litres/2½ pints of water. Bring to the boil, then skim off any surface scum.
2 Add salt and pepper to taste. Simmer for 1½ hours, covered, skimming the stock 3 or 4 more times during cooking.
3 Strain the stock through clean muslin or a fine sieve. Cool quickly and keep chilled until required.

Makes about 1 litre/1¾ pints

FISH STOCK

1 kg/2 lb fish trimmings
1 small onion, finely chopped
2 leeks, chopped
1 bay leaf
few parsley stalks
few fennel sprigs
piece of lemon rind
200 ml/7 fl oz dry white wine
salt and pepper

1 Place the fish trimmings in a large saucepan with the onion, leeks, bay leaf, parsley and lemon rind. Add 1.2 litres/2 pints of water. Bring to the boil slowly, then skim off any surface scum that forms.
2 Add the wine and salt and pepper to taste, and simmer very gently for 30 minutes, skimming the stock once or twice during cooking.
3 Strain the stock through clean muslin or a fine sieve. Cool quickly and keep chilled until required.

Makes about 1 litre/1¾ pints

CHICKEN STOCK

1 chicken carcass, plus giblets
1 onion, chopped
2 large carrots, peeled and chopped
1 celery stick, chopped
1 bay leaf
few parsley stalks
1 thyme sprig
salt and pepper

1 Remove any skin or fat from the chicken carcass and chop into 3 or 4 pieces. Place in a large saucepan with the giblets, onion, carrots, celery, bay leaf, parsley stalks, thyme and 1.8 litres/3 pints of water.
2 Bring to the boil and skim, removing any scum or fat that rises to the surface. Lower the heat and simmer for 2–2½ hours, skimming the stock once or twice during cooking.
3 Strain the stock through clean muslin or a fine sieve. Cool quickly and keep chilled until required.

Makes about 1 litre/1¾ pints

Soups, Starters and Breads

You don't need to skip the starter just because you are watching your fat intake. Here you will discover light summer first courses, like Red Pepper and Ginger Soup, and warming winter dishes, such as Butternut Squash and Rosemary Soup. And Catalan Mussels, teamed up with one of the delicious breads at the end of the chapter, would make a perfect lunch or light supper.

Red Pepper and Ginger Soup

Preparation time: 20 minutes, plus cooling
Cooking time: 45 minutes
Oven temperature: 200°C (400°F), Gas Mark 6

- 3 red peppers, halved, cored and deseeded
- 1 red onion, quartered
- 2 garlic cloves, unpeeled
- 1 teaspoon olive oil
- 5 cm/2 inch piece of fresh root ginger, grated
- 1 teaspoon ground cumin
- 1 teaspoon ground coriander
- 1 large potato, chopped
- 900 ml/1½ pints fresh vegetable stock (see page 9)
- 4 tablespoons low-fat fromage frais
- salt and pepper

1 Place the peppers, onion and garlic cloves in a nonstick roasting tin. Roast in a preheated oven, 200°C (400°F), Gas Mark 6, for *40 minutes*, or until the peppers have blistered and the onion quarters and garlic are very soft. If the onion quarters start to brown too much, cover them with the pepper halves.

2 Meanwhile, heat the oil in a saucepan and fry the ginger, cumin and coriander over a low heat for *5 minutes*, until softened. Add the potato and stir well, season and pour in the vegetable stock. Simmer covered for *30 minutes*.

3 Remove the cooked vegetables from the oven. Place the peppers in a polythene bag. Tie the top and leave to cool. (The steam produced in the bag makes it easier to remove the skin when cool.) Add the onions to the potato mixture and carefully squeeze out the garlic pulp into the saucepan, too. Peel the peppers and add all but one half to the soup. Simmer for *5 minutes*.

4 Pour the soup into a blender or food processor and blend, in batches if necessary, for a few seconds until quite smooth. Return to the saucepan and thin with a little water, if necessary, to achieve the desired consistency.

5 Spoon into warmed bowls. Slice the remaining pepper and lay on top of the soup with a spoonful of fromage frais.

Serves 4
kcal 112; KJ 473; Protein 6 g; Fat 2 g; CHO 21 g

variation _____

Red Pepper and Spicy Chicken Soup

Preparation time: 20 minutes, plus cooling
Cooking time: 45 minutes
Oven temperature: 200°C (400°F), Gas Mark 6

- ingredients as above
- 2 teaspoons five-spice powder
- 150 g/5 oz boneless, skinless chicken breast

1 Make the soup following the main recipe and, while the peppers are roasting, scatter the five-spice powder over the chicken breast and grill under a medium heat for *20 minutes* until crisp.

2 When cooked, cut the chicken into thin shreds. Stir into the pepper soup and simmer for *5 minutes* before serving.

Serves 4
kcal 156; KJ 657; Protein 14 g; Fat 3 g; CHO 21 g

Butternut Squash and Rosemary Soup

Preparation time: 15 minutes
Cooking time: 1 hour 10 minutes
Oven temperature: 200°C (400°F), Gas Mark 6

- **1 butternut squash**
- **few sprigs of rosemary, plus extra, to garnish**
- **150 g/5 oz red lentils, washed**
- **1 onion, finely chopped**
- **900 ml/1½ pints fresh vegetable stock (see page 9)**
- **salt and pepper**

1 Halve the squash and, using a spoon, scoop out the seeds and fibrous flesh. Cut the squash into smaller chunks and place in a roasting tin. Sprinkle over the rosemary and season with salt and pepper. Roast in a preheated oven, 200°C (400°F), Gas Mark 6, for *45 minutes*.

2 Meanwhile, place the lentils in a saucepan. Cover with water, bring to the boil and boil rapidly for *10 minutes*. Strain, then return the lentils to a clean saucepan with the onion and stock and simmer for *5 minutes*. Season to taste.

3 Remove the squash from the oven and scoop out the flesh, mash with a fork and add to the soup. Simmer for *25 minutes* and then ladle into bowls. Garnish with more rosemary before serving.

Serves 4
kcal 145; KJ 614; Protein 10 g; Fat 1 g; CHO 26 g

Roast Root Vegetable Soup

Preparation time: 10 minutes
Cooking time: 1 hour 5 minutes
Oven temperature: 200°C (400°F), Gas Mark 6

- 4 carrots, chopped
- 2 parsnips, chopped
- 1 leek, very finely chopped
- 1.2 litres/2 pints fresh
  vegetable stock (see page 9)

- 2 teaspoons thyme leaves
- salt and pepper
- sprigs of thyme, to garnish

1 Place the carrots and parsnips in a roasting tin and season with salt and pepper. Roast in a preheated oven, 200°C (400°F), Gas Mark 6, for *1 hour*, or until the vegetables are very soft.

2 Meanwhile, *20 minutes* before the vegetables have finished roasting, put the leeks in a large saucepan with the stock and 1 teaspoon of the thyme. Simmer, covered, for *20 minutes*.

3 Transfer the roasted root vegetables to a blender or food processor and blend, adding a little of the stock if necessary. Transfer to the saucepan and check the seasoning. Add the remaining thyme, stir and simmer for *5 minutes*.

4 Ladle into warmed bowls and serve garnished with the thyme sprigs.

Serves 6
kcal 60; KJ 254; Protein 2 g; Fat 1 g; CHO 12 g

Mushroom Hot and Sour Soup

Preparation time: 5 minutes
Cooking time: 15 minutes

- 1.2 litres/2 pints fresh fish stock (see page 9)
- 1 lemon grass stalk, lightly crushed
- 3 fresh kaffir lime leaves or 3 pieces of lime peel
- 2 Thai red chillies, halved and deseeded
- 2 tablespoons lime juice
- 2 tablespoons Thai fish sauce
- 50 g/2 oz canned bamboo shoots
- 125 g/4 oz oyster mushrooms
- 2 spring onions, finely sliced
- ½ red chilli, sliced, to garnish

1 Pour the fish stock into a saucepan, add the lemon grass, lime leaves or peel and chillies. Simmer for *10 minutes*.

2 Strain the liquid into a clean saucepan. Reserve a little red chilli and discard the remaining seasonings.

3 Add the lime juice and fish sauce to the stock with the bamboo shoots and mushrooms and reserved chilli; simmer for *5 minutes*. Spoon into warmed bowls and sprinkle with the spring onions. Garnish with red chilli slices and serve.

Serves 4
kcal 23; KJ 97; Protein 2 g; Fat 0 g; CHO 3 g

Spring Vegetable Broth

Preparation time: 5 minutes
Cooking time: 40 minutes

- 2 teaspoons olive oil
- 2 celery sticks with their
  leaves, chopped
- 2 leeks, chopped
- 1 carrot, finely diced
- 50 g/2 oz pearl barley
- 1.2 litres/2 pints fresh
  vegetable stock (see page 9)
- 125 g/4 oz mangetout,
  diagonally sliced
- salt and pepper

1 Heat the oil in a saucepan and add the chopped celery and leaves, leeks and carrot. Cook over a medium heat for *10 minutes*.

2 Stir in the pearl barley and stock, season to taste and simmer for *20 minutes*. Add the mangetout and simmer for *10 minutes*. Ladle into warmed bowls and serve.

Serves 4
kcal 76; KJ 322; Protein 3 g; Fat 2 g; CHO 13 g

variation _____
Hearty Lamb Broth

Preparation time: 5 minutes
Cooking time: 35 minutes

1 Make the soup, following the main recipe, but replace the mangetout with 125 g/4 oz shredded, cooked lean lamb. Cook for *5 minutes* and serve.

Serves 4
kcal 134; KJ 562; Protein 11 g; Fat 5 g; CHO 13 g

Carrot and Coriander Pâté

Preparation time: 5 minutes, plus chilling
Cooking time: 40 minutes

- 500 g/1 lb carrots, grated
- 1 tablespoon ground coriander
- 175 ml/6 fl oz freshly squeezed orange juice
- 300 ml/½ pint water
- 50 g/2 oz medium-fat soft cheese
- 30 g/1¼ oz fresh coriander leaves
- salt and pepper

1 Place the grated carrot in a saucepan with the ground coriander, orange juice and water. Cover with a lid and simmer for *40 minutes* until the carrots are cooked. Cool and transfer to a blender or food processor with a little of the cooking liquid.

2 Add the soft cheese and coriander leaves; blend until smooth. Season to taste and blend again. Spoon into small dishes and chill before serving with country bread.

Serves 4
kcal 84; KJ 353; Protein 2 g; Fat 2 g; CHO 14 g

variation

Chickpea and Carrot Pâté

Preparation time: 5 minutes, plus chilling
Cooking time: 40 minutes

1 Follow the main recipe, replacing the coriander leaves with a 275 g/9 oz can of drained chickpeas. Blend until smooth. Spoon into small dishes and chill until ready to serve.

Serves 4
kcal 154; KJ 647; Protein 7 g; Fat 4 g; CHO 24 g

Baked Field Mushrooms

Preparation time: 5 minutes
Cooking time: 40 minutes
Oven temperature: 200°C (400°F), Gas Mark 6

- 5 large field or open cap mushrooms
- 4 tablespoons balsamic vinegar
- 1 tablespoon wholegrain mustard
- 75 g/3 oz watercress
- sea salt and pepper
- Parmesan shavings, to garnish (optional)

1 Remove the stalks from 4 of the mushrooms and reserve. Place the 4 mushrooms in a small roasting tin, skin side down. Cook in a preheated oven, 200°C (400°F), Gas Mark 6, for *15 minutes*.

2 Meanwhile, make the dressing. Finely chop the remaining mushroom and reserved stalks and mix in a small bowl with the vinegar and mustard. Season with salt and pepper.

3 Remove the mushrooms from the oven and spoon the dressing over each mushroom. Return to the oven and continue to cook for *25 minutes*, covering the tin with foil after *10 minutes*.

4 When cooked, lift the mushrooms on to a plate and keep warm. Tip the watercress into the hot juices and toss well. Spoon piles of watercress on to 4 warmed plates. Place a mushroom on top and garnish with Parmesan, if liked.

Serves 4
kcal 42; KJ 177; Protein 4 g; Fat 3 g; CHO 1 g

Chive and Onion Bread

Preparation time: 20 minutes, plus rising
Cooking time: 20–30 minutes
Oven temperature: 220°C (425°F), Gas Mark 7

- 500 g/1 lb strong plain flour
- 5 g/¼ oz sachet easy-blend dried yeast
- 1 teaspoon salt
- 15 g/½ oz low-fat margarine
- 300–400 ml/½ pint–14 fl oz warm water
- 1 bunch of chives, snipped
- 1 onion, finely chopped
- sea salt, for sprinkling

1 Sift the flour into a large bowl, add the yeast and salt. Rub in the fat and then make a well in the centre. Pour in the water and bring the mixture together with a round-bladed knife.

2 Turn out the dough on to a floured surface and knead for *10 minutes*, or until the dough is soft and elastic. Place the dough in a clean bowl and cover with a damp tea towel. Leave to rise in a warm place for *1 hour*, or until it has doubled in size.

3 Tip out the dough on to a floured surface and knock back (see page 26). Knead for *5 minutes*, then work in the chives and onion. Transfer the dough to a 23 x 15 cm/9 x 6 inch nonstick roasting tin. Flatten the dough out with your hands and then cover with a damp cloth and leave to rise for *1 hour*, or until doubled in size again.

4 When risen, make dents all over the surface with your finger or the end of a wooden spoon. Scatter with sea salt and bake in a preheated oven, 220°C (425°F), Gas Mark 7, for *20–30 minutes*, or until golden and the base sounds hollow when tapped.

Makes a 750g/1½ lb loaf (12 slices)
Per slice: kcal 150; KJ 644; Protein 5 g; Fat 1 g; CHO 32 g

Catalan Mussels

Preparation time: 10 minutes
Cooking time: 15 minutes

- 1 tablespoon olive oil
- 1 onion, finely chopped
- 2 garlic cloves, crushed
- 1 red chilli, deseeded and finely chopped
- pinch of paprika
- 400 g/13 oz can chopped tomatoes
- 1 kg/2 lb mussels
- salt and pepper
- parsley, chopped, to garnish

1 Heat the oil in a large saucepan or wok. Fry the onion, garlic, chilli and paprika over a medium heat for *10 minutes* or until soft. Stir in the tomatoes and season. Cover and simmer over a low heat while you clean the mussels.

2 Pull the beards from the mussels and scrub the shells. Discard any shells that remain open after you have tapped them on the work surface or any that are broken.

3 Stir the mussels into the tomato sauce, increase the temperature and cover with a lid. Cook for *5 minutes* until the shells have opened. (Discard any mussels that remain closed.)

4 Pile into warmed serving bowls, sprinkle with chopped parsley, and serve.

Serves 4
kcal 119; KJ 498; Protein 15 g; Fat 4 g; CHO 6 g

variation _____

Mussels with a Herb Crust

Preparation time: 10 minutes
Cooking time: 20–25 minutes

- ingredients as above, except the tomatoes
- 50 g/2 oz fresh wholemeal breadcrumbs
- 2 teaspoons chopped mixed herbs
- lemon slices, to garnish

1 Follow the main recipe, omitting the tomatoes and adding a little water in their place.

2 Once the mussels (green-lipped ones are best for this) are cooked, discard the empty half of each shell. Put the opened mussels on a baking sheet. If there is quite a lot of liquid left in the pan, boil rapidly for *5 minutes* until the mixture has almost evaporated.

3 Mix the breadcrumbs and the mixed herbs together with the onion mixture in the saucepan, to form a semi-sticky paste. Scatter over the mussels and place under a preheated grill. Cook for *5 minutes*. Garnish with lemon slices.

Serves 4
kcal 130; KJ 544; Protein 15 g; Fat 5 g; CHO 8 g

Storecupboard Ingredients

The right seasonings and ingredients can transform familiar foods into Mexican, Italian or Oriental specialities. Here are a few examples of excellent storecupboard ingredients. Keep a supply of them to hand to enable you to create delicious low fat meals any time.

Sun-dried tomato paste

Capers

Caperberries

Green peppercorns

Beetroot

Ground cumin

Sun-dried tomatoes

Mandarin oranges

Ground cumin has a strong, aromatic taste and is widely used in Indian, Mexican and Oriental dishes.
Sun-dried tomato paste makes an excellent addition to sauces, salads and pasta.
Beetroot has a striking ruby red colour and is available

canned and pickled or fresh.
Capers are pickled in vinegar or salted and can be served whole or chopped.
Caperberries are the larger caper buds imported from Spain. Available in jars.
Sun-dried tomatoes are tomatoes that have been cut

and then dried in the sun to intensify and sweeten the natural flavour.
Mandarin oranges are small citrus fruits with flesh that separates easily into segments and skin that does not cling tightly to the fruit.
Green peppercorns are

pepper berries preserved in brine before they are fully ripe; they are milder and fruitier than black peppercorns.
Green Thai curry paste has the flavour of lemon grass and green chillies; add to stir-fries and marinades.
Sesame seeds can be

Thai curry paste

Poppy seeds

Cajun seasoning

Sesame seeds

Bamboo shoots

Vermicelli

Bean thread noodles

Sea salt

Pumpkin seeds

Ground coriander

Cinnamon sticks

sprinkled over breads or salads for a nutty taste.

Pumpkin seeds can be eaten raw or cooked in sweet or savoury foods; high in fibre.

Poppy seeds have a nutty flavour and make an attractive topping on breads or salads.

Sea salt has no artificial additives and its strong taste means less is required.

Cajun seasoning is an excellent seasoning and can be dry-fried to give a typical blackened look.

Bamboo shoots are more often found canned than fresh. They add a wonderful crunchy texture to dishes.

Ground coriander has a pleasant, mild aroma and slightly peppery taste; often used in curries.

Vermicelli is thin spaghetti. Classic pastas are naturally low in fat; wholewheat pastas are richer in vitamins, minerals and contain more dietary fibre.

Bean thread noodles, or cellophane or transparent noodles, are made from ground mung beans.

Cinnamon sticks are one of the most popular spices but are often mistaken for their close relative, cassia bark.

Five-Seed Rolls

Preparation time: 20 minutes, plus rising
Cooking time: 15 minutes
Oven temperature: 220°C (425°F), Gas Mark 7

- 250 g/8 oz strong plain flour
- 1 teaspoon salt
- 1 teaspoon easy-blend dried
  yeast
- 1 teaspoon sunflower seeds
- 1 teaspoon poppy seeds
- 1 teaspoon pumpkin seeds
- 1 teaspoon sesame seeds
- 1 teaspoon cumin seeds
- 150–200 ml/¼ pint–7 fl oz
  skimmed milk, warmed
- plain flour, for dusting

1 Sift the flour into a large bowl. Stir in the salt and the yeast, then stir in the seeds.

2 Make a well in the centre of the bowl and stir in the warm milk. Bring the mixture together then knead well on a lightly floured surface for *10 minutes*, or until the dough is smooth and elastic. Return to a clean bowl. Cover with a damp tea towel and leave to rise in a warm place for *1 hour*, or until the dough has doubled in size.

3 Tip out the dough on to a floured surface and knock back. (Knocking back means kneading with your knuckles to knock out the air bubbles and produce a more even texture.) Divide the dough into 8 and shape into even rolls. Transfer to a nonstick baking sheet and cover with a damp tea towel again. Leave to rise in a warm place for *1 hour* or until the dough has doubled in size again.

4 Bake in a preheated oven, 220°C (425°F) Gas Mark 7, for *10 minutes*. Dust the part-baked rolls with flour and return to the oven for another *5 minutes*. The rolls are cooked when evenly browned and the bases sound hollow when tapped.

Makes 8
Per roll: kcal 131; KJ 558; Protein 5 g; Fat 2 g; CHO 26 g

Simple Milk Bread

Preparation time: 30 minutes, plus rising
Cooking time: 25 minutes
Oven temperature: 220°C (425°F), Gas Mark 7

- **500 g/1 lb strong plain flour**
- **1 teaspoon salt**
- **5 g/¼ oz sachet easy-blend dried yeast**
- **pinch of caster sugar**
- **15 g/½ oz low-fat margarine**
- **300–350 ml/½ pint–12 fl oz skimmed milk, warmed**
- **sea salt, for sprinkling**

1 Sift the flour into a large bowl. Stir in the salt, yeast and sugar. Rub in the margarine and make a well in the centre. Pour in the milk. Stir and bring the mixture together and then knead on a lightly floured surface for *10 minutes*, or until smooth and elastic.

2 Place the dough in a clean bowl. Cover with a damp tea towel and leave to rise for *1 hour*, or until doubled in size.

3 Tip the risen dough out on to a floured surface, knock back (see page 26) and knead for *5 minutes*.

4 Divide the dough into three pieces and roll each one out to form a 20 cm/8 inch long sausage shape. Join the three pieces together at one end and then turn the pieces so that the joined end is furthest away from you. Plait the three sausages over and under each other towards you and then join the ends together when you run out of dough.

5 Lift on to a nonstick baking sheet and cover with a damp tea towel again. Leave to rise in a warm place until the dough has doubled in size again. When risen, brush the bread with a little more skimmed milk. Sprinkle the loaf with sea salt.

6 Bake in a preheated oven, 220°C (425°F), Gas Mark 7, for *25 minutes*, or until the loaf is golden and sounds hollow when tapped.

Makes a 750 g/1½ lb loaf (18 slices)
Per slice: kcal 106; KJ 450; Protein 3 g; Fat 1 g; CHO 23 g

Pesto Twists

Preparation time: 20 minutes, plus rising
Cooking time: 15 minutes
Oven temperature: 220°C (425°F), Gas Mark 7

- 250 g/8 oz strong plain flour
- ½ teaspoon salt
- 1 teaspoon easy-blend dried yeast
- 150 ml/¼ pint warm water
- handful of basil leaves
- 1 teaspoon pine nuts
- 1 teaspoon grated Parmesan cheese

1 Sift the flour into a large bowl, add the salt and yeast. Pour the water into a blender or food processor and add the remaining ingredients, except those in the bowl. Blend for a few seconds to form a runny paste.

2 Make a well in the centre of the flour and stir in the paste, bringing the mixture together with a round-bladed knife. The dough will be quite wet, so turn it out on to a well-floured surface and knead for *10 minutes*, until the dough is soft and elastic. Place the dough in a clean bowl. Cover with a damp tea towel and leave to rise in a warm place for *1 hour*, or until doubled in size.

3 Tip out the dough on to a floured surface and knock back (see page 26), then knead for *5 minutes*. Divide the dough into 8 pieces. Roll each piece into a long thin sausage shape. Tie each sausage into a knot and place on a nonstick baking sheet. Cover the twists with a damp cloth and leave to rise for *1 hour*, or until doubled in size again.

4 Bake in a preheated oven, 220°C (425°F), Gas Mark 7, for *15 minutes*, or until the twists sound hollow when tapped on the base.

Makes 8
Per twist: kcal 115; KJ 490; Protein 4 g; Fat 1 g; CHO 24 g

variation _____

Red Pesto Twists

Preparation time: 20 minutes, plus rising
Cooking time: 15 minutes
Oven temperature: 220°C (425°F), Gas Mark 7

- 250 g/8 oz strong plain flour
- ½ teaspoon salt
- 1 teaspoon easy-blend dried yeast
- 150 ml/¼ pint warm water
- 2 teaspoons red pesto
- grated Parmesan cheese, for sprinkling

1 Make the dough as in the main recipe, omitting the basil, pine nuts and Parmesan. Instead, combine the water with the red pesto and work into the dough. Continue as for the main recipe, kneading and proving the dough and making the twists.

2 Before baking, sprinkle the twists with a little Parmesan.

Makes 8
Per twist: kcal 117; KJ 497; Protein 4 g; Fat 1 g; CHO 25 g

Poultry, Game and Meat

Tasty food does not have to be fatty food, as this chapter will prove. Herbs and spices are used creatively in tempting dishes such as Lime and Ginger Suprêmes and Green Beef Curry. Old favourites like Green Peppercorn Steak are given added interest with soy sauce and balsamic vinegar. Also included are chicken, rabbit and even ostrich – there really is something for everyone.

Mandarin Chicken

Preparation time: 5 minutes, plus marinating
Cooking time: 20 minutes

- **500 g/1 lb boneless, skinless chicken breast, diced**
- **300 g/10 oz can mandarin segments in juice, drained and juice reserved**
- **grated rind and juice of 1 lemon**
- **4 spring onions, shredded**
- **2 tablespoons Thai seven-spice seasoning**
- **1 tablespoon dark soy sauce**

1 Place the diced chicken in a bowl with the mandarin juice, lemon rind and juice, spring onions, seven-spice seasoning and soy sauce. Stir to combine and leave to marinate, covered, in a refrigerator for at least *1 hour* or overnight.

2 Before cooking, soak 4 wooden skewers in warm water for *10 minutes*, then drain.

3 Thread the chicken and mandarin segments on to the skewers, packing them tightly together so the fruit does not fall off. Place under a preheated medium grill and cook for *10 minutes*. Turn the skewers, baste with any remaining marinade and cook for a further *10 minutes*. Serve on a bed of low-fat noodles tossed with spring onions and red chillies.

Serves 4
kcal 175; KJ 737; Protein 28 g; Fat 4 g; CHO 7 g

variation ————————————
Citrus Chicken

Preparation time: 5 minutes, plus marinating
Cooking time: 20 minutes

1 Prepare the chicken as in the main recipe, omitting the mandarin segments and spring onions and replacing with a lime. Slice the lime and thread on to the skewers with the chicken. Cook as for the main recipe.

Serves 4
kcal 150; KJ 633; Protein 28 g; Fat 4 g; CHO 1 g

Lime and Ginger Suprêmes

Preparation time: 5 minutes, plus standing
Cooking time: 20–30 minutes

- 4 chicken suprêmes, about 150 g/5 oz each
- 1 lime, halved and thinly sliced
- 2.5 cm/1 inch piece of fresh root ginger, grated
- 2 tablespoons light soy sauce
- 2 tablespoons dry sherry
- 1 red chilli, deseeded and finely sliced
- flat leaf parsley sprigs, to garnish

1 Remove and discard the skin from each chicken suprême. Make a few deep cuts through the meat, making sure not to cut all the way through the breast. Push a slice of lime into each slit and lift the chicken on to a grill rack.

2 In a bowl mix together the ginger, soy sauce, sherry and chilli. Brush over each chicken suprême and leave to stand for *10 minutes*.

3 Place under a preheated medium grill and cook for *20–30 minutes* or until the juices run clear, covering the meat with foil if necessary to prevent it from over-browning. Warm the remaining marinade and drizzle over the chicken before serving. Garnish with flat leaf parsley and serve with steamed vegetables.

Serves 4
kcal 190; KJ 800; Protein 34 g; Fat 5 g; CHO 1 g

Carnival Chicken with Sweet Potato Mash

Preparation time: 15–20 minutes, plus marinating
Cooking time: 20 minutes

- 4 skinless chicken breasts, about 150 g/5 oz each
- flat leaf parsley sprigs, to garnish

MARINADE:

- 100 ml/3½ fl oz sweet sherry
- 1 teaspoon Angostura bitters
- 1 tablespoon light soy sauce
- 1 tablespoon chopped fresh root ginger
- pinch of ground cumin
- pinch of ground coriander
- 1 teaspoon dried mixed herbs
- 1 small onion, finely chopped
- 75 ml/3 fl oz fresh chicken stock (see page 9)

SWEET POTATO MASH:

- 2 sweet potatoes
- 2 tablespoons very low-fat fromage frais (optional)
- salt and pepper

1 Place the chicken breasts in a non-metallic dish. In a bowl mix together all the marinade ingredients. Spoon over the chicken, making sure the pieces are well coated. Cover and leave to marinate in the refrigerator overnight.

2 When you are ready to cook, place the chicken on a grill pan and cook under a preheated medium grill for *20 minutes*, turning over halfway through cooking.

3 Meanwhile, boil the sweet potatoes in their skins for *20 minutes*, until soft. Drain well and peel. Mash the potato and let it dry off a bit then stir in the fromage frais, if using. Season and serve with the chicken. Garnish with the flat leaf parsley.

Serves 4
kcal 315; KJ 1332; Protein 36 g; Fat 5 g; CHO 26 g

Blackened Chicken Skewers

Preparation time: 5 minutes, plus marinating
Cooking time: 20 minutes

- 300 g/10 oz skinless chicken breast, diced
- 1 tablespoon Cajun seasoning mix
- 2 tablespoons lemon juice
- 1 teaspoon olive oil
- coriander sprigs, to garnish

1 Place the chicken in a bowl and add the seasoning mix, lemon juice and olive oil. Toss well and leave to marinate for *15 minutes*. Meanwhile, soak 8 wooden skewers in warm water.

2 Drain the skewers and thread the pieces of chicken on to them. Cover the ends of the skewers with foil, place under a preheated medium grill and cook for *20 minutes*, turning over halfway through cooking. When the chicken is cooked through, remove from the grill and reserve any juices. Remove the chicken from the skewers and garnish with coriander sprigs. Serve with the juices, a timbale of boiled rice and a green salad.

Serves 4
kcal 94; KJ 397; Protein 16 g; Fat 3 g; CHO 0 g

Clay Pot Baked Spring Chicken

Preparation time: 15 minutes, plus standing
Cooking time: 1 hour 50 minutes
Oven temperature: 200°C (400°F), Gas Mark 6

- 1.5 kg/3 lb free-range chicken
- 1 lemon, pricked or slashed
- 2 rosemary sprigs, plus extra, to garnish
- 2 red peppers, halved, cored and deseeded
- 2 yellow peppers, halved, cored and deseeded
- 300 ml/½ pint fresh chicken stock (see page 9)
- sea salt and pepper

1 Soak a clay pot for *10 minutes* in cold water. Meanwhile, remove the giblets from the chicken, rinse the cavity and pat the chicken dry with kitchen paper.

2 Push the lemon and rosemary into the chicken cavity. Drain the clay pot of water. Lift the chicken into the pot and lay the pepper pieces around; pour over the chicken stock. Season well. Cover with the clay pot lid.

3 Put the pot into a cold oven and then bake at 200°C (400°F), Gas Mark 6, for *1 hour 50 minutes*.

4 Remove the chicken and peppers from the pot and allow to stand for *10 minutes*. Meanwhile, strain off the fat from the cooking juices by letting them drain through the hole in the clay pot. Pour the cooking liquid into a saucepan and boil rapidly for *5 minutes*.

5 Remove the chicken skin before serving as it is the most fatty part of the bird. Garnish with a wedge of the lemon and fresh rosemary sprigs. Serve with the reduced stock and the peppers.

Serves 4
kcal 155; KJ 654; Protein 23 g; Fat 5 g; CHO 5 g

Turkey Ragoût

Preparation time: 10 minutes
Cooking time: 1 hour 50 minutes
Oven temperature: 180°C (350°F), Gas Mark 4

- 1 turkey drumstick, weighing 625 g/1¼ lb
- 4 garlic cloves
- 15 baby onions or shallots
- 3 carrots, diagonally sliced
- 300 ml/½ pint Burgundy red wine
- few thyme sprigs
- 2 bay leaves
- 2 tablespoons chopped flat leaf parsley
- 1 teaspoon port wine jelly
- 1 teaspoon wholegrain mustard
- salt and pepper

1 Carefully remove the skin from the turkey drumstick. Once the skin is removed make a few slashes in the meat. Finely slice 1 garlic clove into slivers and push into the slashes. Crush the remaining garlic. Place the drumstick into a large flameproof casserole or roasting tin with the onions, carrots, garlic, red wine, thyme and bay leaves. Season well and cover with a lid.

2 Cook in a preheated oven, 180°C (350°F), Gas Mark 4, for about *1¾ hours*.

3 Remove the turkey and vegetables and keep hot. Bring the sauce to the boil on the hob, discarding the bay leaves. Add the parsley, port wine jelly and mustard. Boil for *5 minutes,* until slightly thickened and check and adjust the seasoning. Carve the turkey and serve with the juices.

Serves 4
kcal 190; KJ 800; Protein 20 g; Fat 4 g; CHO 7 g

variation
Turkey Wraps

Preparation time: 30 minutes
Cooking time: 1 hour 20 minutes
Oven temperature: 180°C (350°F), Gas Mark 4

- ingredients as above

1 Carefully bone the drumstick and open out the joint. Chop the onions and carrots and mix together with the garlic. Spoon the vegetables along the boned side of the drumstick. Fold the joint over and tie with string. Place in a casserole or roasting tin and add the wine, thyme and bay leaves.

2 Cook the joint, covered, in a preheated oven, 180°C (350°F), Gas Mark 4, for *1 hour 20 minutes* and then continue, following step 3 of the main recipe.

Serves 4
kcal 190; KJ 800; Protein 20 g; Fat 4 g; CHO 7 g

Herby Rabbit Casserole

Preparation time: 10 minutes
Cooking time: 1 hour 10 minutes

- 375 g/12 oz lean rabbit meat, diced
- 1 tablespoon chopped rosemary, plus 1 sprig, to garnish
- 1 tablespoon mixed herbs
- 1 tablespoon plain flour
- 1 teaspoon olive oil
- 1 red onion, cut into wedges
- 1 piece of orange peel
- 4 sun-dried tomatoes, rehydrated and chopped
- 150 ml/¼ pint red wine
- 50 g/2 oz Puy lentils
- sea salt and pepper

1 Place the meat in a large polythene bag. Add the herbs and flour; toss well to coat the meat.

2 Heat the oil in a large flameproof casserole. Fry the coated meat for a few minutes until browned. Add the onion wedges, orange peel and tomatoes.

3 Pour in the wine and add enough water to just cover the meat. Season well. Cover the casserole with a lid and simmer for *40 minutes–1 hour* or until the meat is very tender and the vegetables are cooked.

4 Meanwhile, *30 minutes* before the end of cooking time, rinse the lentils and cook in a saucepan of boiling water for *20 minutes*. Drain and stir into the casserole. Simmer for *10 minutes*. Remove the orange peel before serving and garnish with a rosemary sprig.

Serves 4
kcal 218; KJ 917; Protein 25 g; Fat 5 g;
CHO 13 g

Fresh Flavours

Adding flavour need not mean adding extra fat. Using fresh ingredients will provide maximum flavour, vitamins and colour for all dishes. Most supermarkets now stock a wonderful selection of exotic foods and flavours from around the world.

Braeburn apples

Strawberries

Thai red chillies

Kaffir lime leaves

Plums

Shredded citrus rind

Okra

Braeburn apples have a crunchy texture and a wonderful flavour that combines sweetness and sharpness.

Strawberries are best eaten at room temperature. If lacking sweetness, sprinkle with sugar. Some believe a sprinkle of black pepper will intensify the flavour as well.

Plums are available in many flavours, colours, and sizes; some are better for cooking than others. Choose firm and blemish-free plums.

Kaffir lime leaves are available fresh or dried. They have a pungent lemony-lime taste and are very popular in Thai dishes.

Citrus rind makes attractive garnishes for sweet and savoury dishes. The zest of oranges, lemons and limes contains an aromatic oil which carries the flavour of the fruit.

Thai red chillies are slightly less fiery than the green version as they become sweeter when ripe. As a general rule, the smaller the chilli, the hotter it is.

Okra is a finger-sized green vegetable with a mild taste. Popular in Caribbean and Creole cooking, it is also used to thicken soups and stews.

Watercress is the most celebrated type of cress as its flavoursome peppery leaves can be eaten raw or cooked.

Rocket is also known as arugula. The young, slender

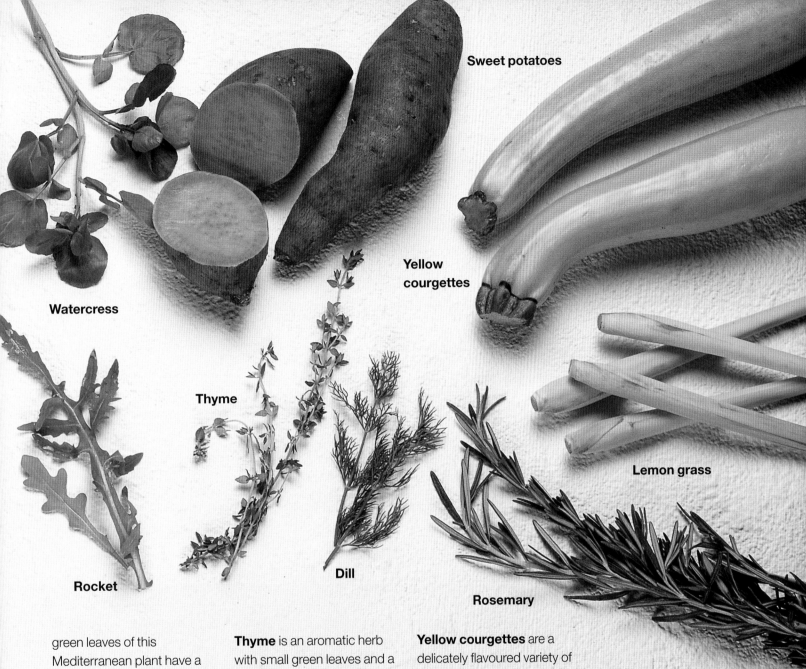

Sweet potatoes

Yellow courgettes

Watercress

Thyme

Lemon grass

Rocket

Dill

Rosemary

green leaves of this Mediterranean plant have a subtle peppery taste and slightly nutty aroma.

Sweet potatoes are not actually potatoes but sweeter, starchy tubers. The three main varieties have either orange, yellow or pink flesh. They should be smooth skinned, firm and blemish free.

Thyme is an aromatic herb with small green leaves and a strong taste. Many varieties are available including lemon thyme (which tastes of lemon) and pretty variegated thyme.

Dill has delicate and feathery fronds with a spicy and refreshing flavour similar to fennel. The dried seeds are used as a spice.

Yellow courgettes are a delicately flavoured variety of marrow. Their intense yellow colour can add interest to many dishes.

Lemon grass is often used in southeast Asian cooking for its lovely lemony flavour with a hint of mint. It is best used fresh although it is available in jars. Use grated lemon zest

mixed with a little finely cut fresh ginger as a substitute.

Rosemary is much better fresh than dried and as it is a very robust herb, only a few leaves are needed to impart high flavour to many dishes.

Spinach-stuffed Chicken Breasts

Preparation time: 20 minutes
Cooking time: 45 minutes
Oven temperature: 190°C (375°F), Gas Mark 5

- **125 g/4 oz fresh spinach leaves**
- **50 g/2 oz very low-fat cream cheese or fromage frais**
- **1 onion, grated**
- **1 teaspoon grated lemon rind**
- **50 g/2 oz chestnut mushrooms, finely chopped**
- **4 skinless chicken breasts, about 150 g/5 oz each**
- **1 large potato, parboiled**
- **sea salt and pepper**

1 Place the spinach and cream cheese or fromage frais in a blender or food processor and blend until smooth. Season well and transfer to a bowl.

2 Dry-fry the grated onion for *5 minutes* until soft and slightly coloured. Add the lemon rind and the mushrooms and fry for a further *5 minutes* to extract the juice from the mushrooms. Stir into the spinach mixture.

3 Make a deep cut along the length of each chicken breast, opening up the slit to form a pocket. Spoon a little of the spinach mixture into each pocket.

4 Finely slice the potato and arrange a quarter of the slices in a line in an ovenproof dish, making sure the potatoes overlap slightly. Lift a chicken breast on to the potatoes. Repeat with the remaining potato and the other three chicken breasts. Season with pepper. Place in a preheated oven, 190°C (375°F), Gas Mark 5, and cook for *45 minutes*, covering with foil if necessary to prevent the chicken from over-browning. Serve with roasted red onions and tomatoes, if liked.

Serves 4
kcal 238; KJ 1002; Protein 37 g; Fat 5 g; CHO 12 g

variation

Chicken Breasts with Puy Lentil and Watercress Stuffing

Preparation time: 20 minutes
Cooking time: 45 minutes
Oven temperature: 190°C (375°F), Gas Mark 5

1 Prepare and cook the chicken as for the main recipe, replacing the spinach with 50 g/2 oz watercress and 50 g/2 oz cooked Puy lentils.

Serves 4
kcal 245; KJ 1035; Protein 38 g; Fat 5 g; CHO 13 g

Ostrich and Wild Mushroom Daube

Preparation time: 5 minutes
Cooking time: 1¼ hours

- 500 g/1 lb lean ostrich meat, diced
- 1 onion, diced
- 2 celery sticks, chopped
- 1 carrot, cut into chunks
- 300 ml/½ pint fresh chicken stock (see page 9)
- 300 ml/½ pint red wine
- 2 bay leaves
- 1 tablespoon tomato purée
- 125 g/4 oz wild mushrooms
- 2 tablespoons torn flat leaf parsley
- salt and pepper

1 Put the meat, onion, celery and carrot into a large flameproof casserole. Add the stock, wine, bay leaves and tomato purée. Stir and season. Cover the casserole and simmer gently for 1¼ hours.

2 15 minutes before the end of cooking time, stir in the mushrooms and simmer until they are tender. Stir in the torn parsley and serve hot.

Serves 4
kcal 310; KJ 1309; Protein 50 g; Fat 5 g; CHO 4 g

Russian Meatballs

Preparation time: 15 minutes, plus chilling
Cooking time: 45 minutes
Oven temperature: 180°C (350°F), Gas Mark 4

- 375 g/12 oz lean minced beef
- 1 onion, roughly chopped
- 1 tablespoon tomato purée
- 1 teaspoon dried mixed
  herbs
- salt and pepper
- chopped parsley, to garnish
- paprika, to sprinkle

SAUCE:
- 1 red onion, finely chopped
- 400 g/13 oz can chopped
  tomatoes
- pinch of paprika
- 1 teaspoon dried mixed
  herbs

1 Place the meat, onion, tomato purée and dried mixed herbs into a blender or food processor. Season well and then blend until smooth. Shape the mixture into 12 balls and chill in the refrigerator for *30 minutes*.

2 Meanwhile, put the sauce ingredients into a saucepan and cook, uncovered, over a low heat for *15–20 minutes*, stirring occasionally. Season to taste. Transfer the sauce to an ovenproof dish and arrange the meatballs on top. Cook in a preheated oven, 180°C (350°F), Gas Mark 4, for *45 minutes*.

3 Serve sprinkled with chopped parsley and paprika.

Serves 4
kcal 154; KJ 650; Protein 21 g; Fat 5 g; CHO 8 g

Green Beef Curry

Preparation time: 5 minutes
Cooking time: 10 minutes

- 300 g/10 oz lean beef fillet, finely sliced
- 1 red onion, cut into thin wedges
- 1–2 tablespoons Thai green curry paste
- 125 g/4 oz mangetout, thinly sliced lengthways
- 150 ml/¼ pint water
- small bunch of basil leaves

1 Preheat a nonstick wok or large frying pan. Dry-fry the beef for *2 minutes*, then remove with a slotted spoon, leaving the juices in the pan.

2 Reheat the pan and stir-fry the onion for *1 minute* until softened. Add the curry paste and stir-fry for another minute or so. Now add the mangetout and water. Return the meat to the pan and stir-fry for a further *5 minutes*. When the beef has cooked, throw in the basil and stir-fry for 30 seconds. Serve immediately with boiled rice, if liked.

Serves 4
kcal 128; KJ 536; Protein 17 g; Fat 5 g; CHO 4 g

variation
Green Chicken with Lime Leaves

Preparation time: 5 minutes
Cooking time: 10 minutes

- 300 g/10 oz skinless chicken breast, diced
- 1 red onion, cut into thin wedges
- 2 tablespoons Thai green curry paste
- 125 g/4 oz mangetout, thinly sliced lengthways
- 150 ml/¼ pint water
- 4 kaffir lime leaves

1 Follow the instructions in the main recipe, substituting the chicken breast for the beef. Add the kaffir lime leaves with the mangetout. Complete as for the main recipe, removing the kaffir lime leaves before serving.

Serves 4
kcal 130; KJ 550; Protein 18 g; Fat 5 g; CHO 4 g

Green Peppercorn Steak

Preparation time: 5 minutes
Cooking time: 6–8 minutes

- 4 lean fillet steaks, weighing
  75 g/3 oz each
- 1 tablespoon green
  peppercorns in brine, drained
- 2 tablespoons light soy sauce

- 1 teaspoon balsamic vinegar
- 8 cherry tomatoes, halved
- thyme sprigs, to garnish

1 Preheat a griddle pan until it is very hot. Cook the steaks for *2–3 minutes* on each side. Remove them from the pan and keep hot.

2 Add the peppercorns, soy sauce, balsamic vinegar and cherry tomatoes to the griddle pan. Allow the liquids to sizzle for *2 minutes*, or until the tomatoes are soft. Spoon the sauce over the steaks and garnish with thyme. Serve with potatoes, if liked.

Serves 4
kcal 130; KJ 548; Protein 17 g; Fat 5 g; CHO 4 g

Fish

Whether you like your fish seared, griddled, stewed, baked or roasted, you will find something here to tempt you. From the fresh flavours of Seared Skate Wings with Caperberries to the Indian-inspired Kerala Prawn Curry, all tastes are catered for. And the bonus is that most of the dishes can be on the table in under half an hour.

Seared Skate Wings with Caperberries

Preparation time: 5 minutes
Cooking time: 6–8 minutes

- 2 skate wings, weighing
  300 g/10 oz each
- 1 teaspoon olive oil
- 2 tablespoons capers, or
  caperberries with their
  stalks, halved lengthways

- 1 tablespoon grated lemon
  rind
- 2 tablespoons lemon juice
- salt and pepper
- lemon wedges, to garnish

1 Cut the skate wings in half and pat dry. Brush each side with a little oil. Heat a griddle pan and sear the skate wings for

3 minutes on each side. If the wings are thick, then cook them for a little longer.

2 Throw the caperberries on top with the lemon rind and juice and cook for a few more seconds. Season and serve garnished with lemon wedges. Serve with steamed ribbons of vegetables, if liked.

Serves 4
kcal 105; KJ 446; Protein 23 g; Fat 1 g; CHO 0 g

Quick Shellfish Stew

Preparation time: 5 minutes
Cooking time: 25 minutes

- 4 shallots, chopped
- 2 celery sticks, finely
  chopped
- 125 ml/4 fl oz white wine
- 1 tablespoon chopped fresh
  mixed herbs
- 400 g/13 oz can plum
  tomatoes
- 500 g/1 lb mixed shellfish
  (such as scallops, mussels,
  tiger prawns, langoustines,
  lobster tails)
- 2 tablespoons chopped dill

1 Dry-fry the shallots and celery in a nonstick saucepan for
1 minute, or until just starting to soften. Add the wine and allow
the mixture to sizzle and reduce by half. Add the mixed herbs.

2 Stir in the tomatoes with their juice. Mash the tomatoes
very slightly and cook for *5 minutes* to reduce slightly. Add the
shellfish and half the dill. Stir once, cover with a lid and simmer
for *15 minutes*. Season and garnish with the remaining
chopped dill. Serve with crusty bread.

Serves 4
kcal 168; KJ 708; Protein 25 g; Fat 3 g; CHO 5 g

Monkfish and Spring Onions Baked in Paper

Preparation time: 15 minutes
Cooking time: 20 minutes
Oven temperature: 200°C (400°F), Gas Mark 6

- 2 monkfish tails, weighing 300 g/10 oz each, bone removed
- ½ bunch of spring onions, diagonally sliced
- 1 tablespoon dry sherry or fish sauce
- 1 lime, pared and sliced
- 1 small green chilli, deseeded and chopped
- salt and pepper

1 Take a large square of baking paper and use it to line a roasting tin. Lay the monkfish in the centre of the paper and top with the spring onions, sherry or fish sauce, pared lime rind and green chilli. Season with a little salt and pepper. Push the lime slices under the fish.

2 Loosely wrap the fish in the paper and cook in a preheated oven, 200°C (400°F), Gas Mark 6, for *20 minutes*, or until the fish is just cooked. Cut into wedges and garnish with the spring onions and juices. Serve with pasta twists and red pepper, if liked.

Serves 4
kcal 112; KJ 476; Protein 24 g; Fat 1 g; CHO 1 g

variation
Cod with Baby Onions and Lemons

Preparation time: 25 minutes
Cooking time: 15–20 minutes
Oven temperature: 200°C (400°F), Gas Mark 6

- 500 g/1 lb piece of cod fillet
- 1 lemon, pared and sliced
- 300 ml/½ pint fresh fish stock (see page 9)
- 2 celery sticks, chopped
- 5 baby onions
- ½ bunch of spring onions, diagonally sliced
- 2 tablespoons dry sherry
- 1 small green chilli, deseeded and chopped
- salt and pepper
- parsley, to garnish

1 Cut the cod into large chunks and thread on to skewers with the slices of lemon. Place in a small roasting tin and set aside while you make the stock.

2 Pour the fish stock into a frying pan. Add the celery and baby onions, boil rapidly for *10 minutes* or until the stock has reduced by half. Pour over the cod, add the lemon rind and the remaining ingredients and season.

3 Cook in a preheated oven, 200°C (400°F), Gas Mark 6, for *15–20 minutes*. Serve garnished with parsley.

Serves 4
kcal 106; KJ 449; Protein 22 g; Fat 1 g; CHO 2 g

Cod Fillets with a Herb Crust

Preparation time: 10 minutes
Cooking time: 20 minutes
Oven temperature: 180°C (350°F), Gas Mark 4

- 4 cod fillets, weighing 125 g/4 oz each
- salt and pepper
- 50 g/2 oz wholemeal breadcrumbs
- 2 tablespoons chopped dill
- 2 tablespoons chopped parsley
- 2 tablespoons chopped chives
- 2 tablespoons very low-fat fromage frais
- 2 plum tomatoes, finely diced
- 2 tablespoons lemon juice

1 Wipe the cod fillets and season with salt and pepper. Place in a foil-lined roasting tin, skin side down.

2 In a bowl mix together the crust ingredients and spoon some on top of each cod fillet, packing down gently.

3 Cook in a preheated oven, 180°C (350°F), Gas Mark 4, for *20 minutes*, covering with foil if the crust is over-browning. Serve with French beans.

Serves 4
kcal 137; KJ 583; Protein 24 g; Fat 1 g; CHO 7 g

variation
Salmon with Herb Sauce

Preparation time: 5 minutes
Cooking time: 6–8 minutes

1 Cook 4 x 50 g/2 oz salmon steaks under a moderate grill for 4 minutes on each side. Combine 1 tablespoon each chopped basil and tarragon and 175 ml/6 fl oz natural yogurt; season. Serve the salmon with the sauce and lemon wedges.

Serves 4
kcal 96; KJ 402; Protein 10 g; Fat 6 g; CHO 2 g

Grilled Sardines with Tabbouleh

Preparation time: 10 minutes
Cooking time: 15 minutes

- 125 g/4 oz bulgar wheat
- 1 onion, finely chopped
- 2 ripe tomatoes, skinned and deseeded
- 1 tablespoon lemon juice
- 1 teaspoon grated lemon rind
- small handful of mint leaves
- 4 small sardines, gutted and boned
- salt and pepper

TO GARNISH:
- lemon wedges
- salad or herb leaves

1 Bring a small saucepan of water to the boil and add the bulgar wheat. Simmer for *5 minutes*, then drain and refresh under cold water. Drain again and put into a bowl. Meanwhile, dry-fry the onion for *5 minutes*.

2 Add the onion, tomatoes, lemon juice and rind to the bulgar wheat. Set aside 4 mint leaves and chop the remainder. Stir the chopped mint into the bulgar wheat mixture; season well.

3 Open out each sardine and lay a mint leaf along the centre. Spoon a little of the tabbouleh over and then carefully fold the fillet back over.

4 Grill the sardines for *5 minutes* and then carefully turn over and grill the other sides for a further *5 minutes*. Serve with the remaining (hot or cold) tabbouleh, garnished with lemon wedges and a few salad or herb leaves.

Serves 4
kcal 209; KJ 877; Protein 14 g; Fat 5 g; CHO 27 g

Griddled Tuna with Shallot Jus

Preparation time: 5 minutes
Cooking time: 15 minutes

- **4 tuna steaks, weighing 100 g/3½ oz each**
- **flat leaf parsley sprigs, to garnish**

SAUCE:
- **4 shallots, finely chopped**
- **300 ml/½ pint red wine**
- **150 ml/¼ pint Marsala**
- **salt and pepper**

1 Preheat a griddle or frying pan until it is very hot. Cook the tuna steaks, 2 at a time for *3 minutes* on each side. Remove from the pan and keep warm.

2 For the sauce, mix the shallots and wines in a separate saucepan, season and boil rapidly until reduced by half. Return the tuna steaks to the pan, add the shallot jus and simmer for *2 minutes*. Garnish with the parsley and serve with mashed potatoes and lime wedges, if liked.

Serves 4
kcal 240; KJ 1000; Protein 24 g; Fat 5 g; CHO 4 g

variation

Griddled Tuna with Quick Tomato Sauce

Preparation time: 5 minutes
Cooking time: 22 minutes

- **4 tuna steaks, weighing 100 g/3½ oz each**

SAUCE:
- **4 plum tomatoes**
- **1 teaspoon garlic purée**
- **1 tablespoon tomato purée**
- **1 tablespoon chopped parsley**
- **salt and pepper**

1 Cook the tuna steaks and set aside, following step 1 of the main recipe.

2 To make the tomato sauce, put all the sauce ingredients into a blender or food processor and blend for *1 minute*. Transfer to a saucepan and cook, uncovered, for *10 minutes*. Season and spoon over the cooked tuna.

Serves 4
kcal 153; KJ 644; Protein 25 g; Fat 5 g; CHO 3 g

Kerala Prawn Curry

Preparation time: 5 minutes
Cooking time: 8 minutes

- ½ teaspoon ground turmeric
- 500 g/1 lb large cooked
  peeled prawns
- 1 teaspoon vegetable oil
- 1 red onion, cut into fine
  wedges
- 2 green chillies, deseeded
  and sliced

- 10 curry leaves (optional)
- 100 ml/3½ fl oz coconut milk
- 2 tablespoons lime juice
- few coriander leaves
- salt and pepper

1 Sprinkle the turmeric over the prawns and set aside. Heat the oil in a wok and stir-fry the onion wedges and chillies until softened.

2 Add the prawns, curry leaves and coconut milk. Simmer for *5 minutes*.

3 Sprinkle over the lime juice and season to taste. Scatter with coriander leaves and stir once. Serve immediately.

Serves 4
kcal 159; KJ 670; Protein 29 g; Fat 3 g; CHO 4 g

Masala Roast Cod

Preparation time: 15 minutes
Cooking time: 30 minutes
Oven temperature: 200°C (400°F), Gas Mark 6

- **1 red chilli, chopped**
- **2 garlic cloves, chopped**
- **1 teaspoon minced ginger**
- **1 teaspoon mustard seeds**
- **large pinch of turmeric**
- **2 cloves**
- **2 cardamoms**
- **5 peppercorns**
- **3 tablespoons water**

- **1 teaspoon olive oil**
- **3 tablespoons low-fat yogurt**
- **25 g/1 oz breadcrumbs**
- **500 g/1 lb piece of cod fillet**
- **250 g/8 oz ripe tomatoes, chopped**

TO GARNISH:

- **lemon wedges and rind**
- **coriander leaves**

1 Put the chilli, garlic, ginger, mustard seeds, turmeric, cloves, cardamoms, peppercorns and water into a coffee grinder and blend to form a paste, or use a pestle and mortar.

2 Heat the oil in a small pan and then fry the chilli paste until the oil comes to the surface. Remove from the heat and stir in the yogurt and breadcrumbs.

3 Place the cod in an ovenproof dish and spread the chilli paste over it. Scatter over the tomatoes and cook, covered, in a preheated oven, 200°C (400°F), Gas Mark 6, for *30 minutes*, or until the fish is tender. Serve with the wedges of lemon and boiled rice tossed with coriander and strips of lemon rind.

Serves 4
kcal 150; KJ 640; Protein 26 g; Fat 3 g; CHO 7 g

Cajun Seafood Salad

Preparation time: 5 minutes, plus chilling
Cooking time: 5 minutes

- 8 tiger prawns, cooked
- 250 g/8 oz squid rings, cooked
- 250 g/8 oz green-lipped mussels, cooked
- 1 teaspoon olive oil
- 1 leek, finely shredded
- 2 teaspoons Cajun seasoning
- 1 red pepper, cored, deseeded and finely diced
- salt and pepper
- salad leaves, to serve

1 Mix together the prawns, squid and mussels in a bowl. Season with salt and pepper. Set aside. Heat the olive oil in a small frying pan and fry the leek, Cajun seasoning and diced red pepper for *5 minutes* until soft.

2 Transfer the vegetables to the seafood and toss carefully. Chill the seafood for *2 hours*, before serving with salad leaves.

Serves 4
kcal 107; KJ 448; Protein 18 g; Fat 2 g; CHO 3 g

variation
Cajun Jackets

Preparation time: 12 minutes, plus chilling
Cooking time: 1 hour 35 minutes
Oven temperature: 200°C (400°F), Gas Mark 6

- ingredients as above
- 4 baking potatoes
- 1 egg white
- 2 teaspoons extra Cajun seasoning

1 Follow the main recipe and leave the seafood salad to chill.

2 Wash the potatoes and pat dry with kitchen paper. Prick all over with a fork. Brush the potatoes with a little beaten egg white and then sprinkle with the Cajun seasoning. Bake in a preheated oven, 200°C (400°F), Gas Mark 6, for *1½ hours*. (To reduce the cooking time thread the potatoes on to a metal skewer.)

3 Once cooked, cut a cross in the top of each baked potato. Fill with the chilled seafood and serve on a bed of salad leaves.

Serves 4
kcal 222; KJ 937; Protein 22 g; Fat 3 g; CHO 29 g

Lemon Sole Stuffed with Wild Mushrooms

Preparation time: 20 minutes
Cooking time: 25 minutes
Oven temperature: 200°C (400°F), Gas Mark 6

- 125 g/4 oz wild mushrooms
  (such as chanterelles)
- 5 g/¼ oz butter
- dash of Worcestershire
  sauce
- 25 g/1 oz sun-dried tomato
  paste

- 25 g/1 oz watercress leaves
- 4 lemon sole fillets, weighing
  75 g/3 oz each, skinned
- 3 tablespoons white wine
- salt and pepper
- dill fronds, to garnish

1 Roughly chop or tear the mushrooms and gently cook in a saucepan with the butter until softened. Add the Worcestershire sauce and sun-dried tomato paste and cook for another few minutes. Stir in the watercress leaves and cook until the leaves are wilted then remove the pan from the heat. Season well.

2 Place the sole fillets on a work surface, skinned side uppermost, and divide the filling between them. Starting at the narrowest point, roll up each fillet to enclose the stuffing and secure with a cocktail stick. Arrange the fish in a small roasting tin with the join underneath each roll. Add the wine, season again and cover with foil.

3 Cook in a preheated oven, 200°C (400°F), Gas Mark 6, for *12 minutes* or until the fish is just opaque. Serve garnished with dill fronds.

Serves 4
kcal 100; KJ 420; Protein 14 g; Fat 4 g; CHO 2 g

Singapore Noodles

Preparation time: 5 minutes, plus standing
Cooking time: 10 minutes

- 250 g /8 oz low fat Chinese
  egg thread noodles or
  vermicelli
- 1 teaspoon vegetable oil
- 1 bunch of spring onions,
  diagonally sliced
- 5 cm/2 inch piece of fresh
  root ginger, grated

- 1 tablespoon medium curry
  paste
- 125 g/4 oz frozen peas
- 250 g/8 oz cooked peeled
  prawns, thawed if frozen
- light soy sauce, to serve

1 Break the noodles into a large bowl. Pour over enough boiling water to cover. Stir and toss the noodles in the water and then leave to one side for *6–10 minutes*.

2 Meanwhile, heat a wok and add the oil. Stir-fry the onions and ginger until softened. Stir in the curry paste and stir-fry for a further *2 minutes* to cook the paste. Stir in the peas and prawns. Reduce the heat and cover; cook for *3 minutes*.

3 Drain the noodles and add to the wok, toss well to coat. Serve immediately with the soy sauce.

Serves 4
kcal 350; KJ 1466; Protein 24 g; Fat 5 g;
CHO 53 g

Vegetarian
Main
Courses

Favourite vegetarian dishes are here given the low-fat, high-flavour treatment. Risotto is spiced up with peppery rocket leaves (remember that a good stock is crucial to the success of this dish). Vegetable kebabs are roasted and flavoured with rosemary to give a delicious caramelized result. Throughout you will find colourful dishes to delight vegetarians and non-vegetarians alike.

Rocket Risotto

Preparation time: 5 minutes
Cooking time: 20–25 minutes

- 1 teaspoon olive oil
- 1 onion, finely chopped
- 300 g/10 oz Arborio rice
- 1.2 litres/2 pints fresh
  vegetable stock (see page 9)
- 50 g/2 oz rocket leaves
- salt and pepper

1 Heat the oil in a nonstick frying pan, add the onion and fry for a few minutes until softened. Pour in the rice and stir well to coat the grains.

2 With the pan over a medium heat, gradually add the vegetable stock. Stir continuously while the stock is absorbed into the rice. Keep on adding the stock a little at a time – this will take about *20 minutes*.

3 Stir in the rocket, reserving 4 leaves for garnish, and cook just until the leaves start to wilt. Season to taste and serve each portion garnished with a rocket leaf.

Serves 4
kcal 290; KJ 1222; Protein 6 g; Fat 1 g; CHO 63 g

variation _____

Mangetout Risotto

Preparation time: 5 minutes
Cooking time: 20–25 minutes

1 Follow the main recipe, replacing the rocket with 250 g/8 oz blanched mangetout or sugar snap peas.

Serves 4
kcal 309; KJ 1290; Protein 8 g; Fat 1 g; CHO 65 g

Roasted Vegetable Kebabs

Preparation time: 20 minutes
Cooking time: 45 minutes
Oven temperature: 200°C (400°F), Gas Mark 6

- 1 small sweet potato
- 1 large yellow courgette, cut into 8 chunks
- 1 small red onion, blanched and cut into 4 wedges
- 4 flat mushrooms
- 4 rosemary sprigs with strong stalks
- oil, to drizzle (optional)
- salt and pepper

1 Peel and cut the sweet potato into 2.5 cm/1 inch chunks, then boil for *10 minutes* to soften slightly.

2 Drain the potato and thread the vegetable chunks and mushrooms on to the rosemary stalks. Lay a square of foil on the work surface and place a kebab in the centre. Gather the foil loosely together and repeat with the remaining 3 kebabs. Lay the kebabs on a rack set in a roasting tin.

3 Roast in a preheated oven, 180°C (350°F), Gas Mark 4, for *45 minutes* until charred. Drizzle the vegetables with a little water or oil occasionally to moisten them if necessary. Serve hot with rice noodles, if liked.

Serves 4
kcal 38; KJ 160; Protein 2 g; Fat 0 g; CHO 8 g

Stuffed Tomatoes

Preparation time: 15–20 minutes
Cooking time: 30 minutes
Oven temperature: 200°C (400°F), Gas Mark 6

- **125 g/4 oz couscous**
- **4 beefsteak tomatoes**
- **4 spring onions, diagonally sliced**
- **1 green pepper, grilled, peeled and deseeded**
- **1 tablespoon white wine vinegar**
- **2 tablespoons wholegrain mustard**
- **salt and pepper**
- **dill, to garnish**
- **mixed herb salad, to serve**

1 Place the couscous in a bowl. Pour over enough boiling water to cover, stir and set aside for *10 minutes*. Meanwhile, cut the top away from each tomato. Carefully core and deseed, reserving the tomato flesh. Dry-fry the spring onions in a nonstick pan for *3 minutes*; set aside.

2 Chop the prepared green pepper and stir into the couscous with the spring onions, vinegar, mustard and tomato flesh. Season to taste and then spoon the mixture inside each tomato. Top each tomato with its lid.

3 Put the tomatoes into a small roasting tin and cook in a preheated oven, 200°C (400°F), Gas Mark 6, for *30 minutes*. Garnish with dill and serve with a mixed herb salad.

Serves 4
kcal 105; KJ 440; Protein 4 g; Fat 2 g; CHO 20 g

Mushroom Crêpes

Preparation time: 20–25 minutes
Cooking time: 35 minutes
Oven temperature: 180°C (350°F), Gas Mark 4

- 50 g/2 oz plain flour
- 150 ml/¼ pint skimmed milk
- 1 small egg, beaten
- 1 teaspoon olive oil
- salt and pepper
- flat leaf parsley sprigs, to garnish

FILLING:

- 300 g/10 oz chestnut mushrooms, chopped
- 1 bunch of spring onions, finely chopped
- 1 garlic clove, chopped
- 400 g/13 oz can chopped tomatoes, drained
- 2 tablespoons chopped oregano

1 To make the crêpe batter, place the flour, milk, egg and seasoning in a blender or food processor and blend until smooth, or whisk by hand.

2 Pour a few drops of oil in a frying pan. Heat the pan and pour in a ladleful of batter and cook for *1 minute*. Carefully flip the pancake and cook the second side. Slide out of the pan on to greaseproof paper. Make 3 more pancakes in the same way, adding a few more drops of oil to the pan between each, and stack in between greaseproof paper.

3 Now make the filling: put all the ingredients into a small saucepan and cook, stirring occasionally, for *5 minutes*. Divide the filling between the pancakes, reserving a little of the mixture to serve, and roll up. Transfer the pancakes to an ovenproof dish and cook in a preheated oven, 180°C (350°F), Gas Mark 4, for *20 minutes*. Serve with the remaining mixture and garnish with the parsley.

Serves 4
kcal 112; KJ 470; Protein 7 g; Fat 3 g; CHO 15 g

variation
Wholemeal Crêpes with Wild Mushrooms

Preparation time: 20–25 minutes
Cooking time: 20 minutes
Oven temperature: 200°C (400°F), Gas Mark 6

- 50 g/2 oz wholemeal flour
- 150 ml/¼ pint skimmed milk
- 1 small egg, beaten
- 1 teaspoon olive oil
- salt and pepper
- flat leaf parsley sprigs, to garnish

FILLING:

- 1 bunch of spring onions, finely chopped
- 1 garlic clove, chopped
- 125 g/4 oz wild mushrooms, torn
- 50 g/2 oz low-fat curd cheese
- 1 tablespoon chopped flat leaf parsley

1 Make and cook the pancakes, following the main recipe, replacing the plain flour with the wholemeal.

2 Make the filling and complete the crêpes, following step 3 of the main recipe.

Serves 4
kcal 106; KJ 444; Protein 6 g; Fat 5 g; CHO 10 g

Leek Filo Tarts

Preparation time: 20 minutes
Cooking time: 30 minutes
Oven temperature: 200°C (400°F), Gas Mark 6

- 8 sun-dried tomatoes
- 2 leeks, sliced into rings
- 300 ml/½ pint white wine
- 2 tablespoons skimmed milk
- 1 small egg, separated
- 50 g/2 oz low-fat soft cheese
- 12 x 15 cm/6 inch squares of filo pastry
- salt and pepper

1 Put the tomatoes into a small bowl and pour over enough boiling water to cover. Set aside for *20 minutes*.

2 Meanwhile, put the leeks into a saucepan with the white wine, bring to the boil and simmer until all of the wine has evaporated. Remove the leeks from the heat and stir in the milk, egg yolk and soft cheese; season well.

3 Brush a pastry square with a little egg white and use it to line the base and sides of a 10 cm/4 inch tart case. Brush two more squares and lay these on top, each at a slightly different angle from the first, allowing the edges to flop over the rim. Line three more tart cases in the same way, using up all the pastry squares.

4 Half-fill each pastry case using a spoonful of the cooked leek mixture. Lay two rehydrated tomatoes on top of each tart and then cover with the remaining leeks. Season well and cook in a preheated oven, 200°C (400°F), Gas Mark 6, for *20 minutes*, covering with aluminium foil after 10 minutes. Serve with vine tomatoes and sliced red onion.

Serves 4
kcal 135; KJ 565; Protein 5 g; Fat 5 g; CHO 7 g

Balti Vegetables

Preparation time: 15 minutes
Cooking time: 35 minutes

- 250 g/8 oz potatoes, roughly
  chopped
- 250 g/8 oz French beans,
  trimmed
- 1 red onion, cut into thin
  wedges
- 1 teaspoon ground cumin
- 1 teaspoon ground coriander
- few cardamoms, crushed

- 1 red chilli, deseeded and
  finely chopped
- 125 g/4 oz okra, sliced into
  chunks
- 2 x 400 g/13 oz cans
  tomatoes
- pinch of garam masala
- salt and pepper
- coriander leaves, to garnish

1 Put the potatoes and beans into a large saucepan. Cover with water and boil for *10 minutes*. Drain, reserving both the vegetables and the liquid.

2 Heat a nonstick wok, and dry-fry the onion for *5 minutes*. Stir in the spices and cook for *1 minute*.

3 Add the potatoes, beans and a little of the cooking liquid to the wok. Stir in the chilli, okra and canned tomatoes with their juice. Simmer for *20 minutes*.

4 Check and adjust the seasoning and add the garam masala. Simmer for *5 minutes* more and serve, garnished with coriander leaves.

Serves 4
kcal 92; KJ 389; Protein 5 g; Fat 1 g; CHO 17 g

Spaghetti with Mixed Herb Dressing

Preparation time: 5 minutes
Cooking time: 12 minutes

- 300 g/10 oz dried angel hair
  spaghetti

DRESSING:

- 2 tablespoons chopped
  oregano leaves
- 2 tablespoons chopped flat
  leaf parsley
- 2 tablespoons balsamic
  vinegar
- 2 tablespoons red wine
  vinegar
- 2 tablespoons orange juice
- 1 small garlic clove, crushed
- 1 tablespoon olive oil
- salt and pepper

1 Bring a large saucepan of salted water to the boil. Cook the pasta for *12 minutes*, or according to packet instructions.

2 Meanwhile, put the dressing ingredients in a small saucepan. Season lightly and bring to the boil, then remove from the heat. Leave to infuse for *5 minutes*.

3 Drain the pasta and return to the saucepan. Pour the dressing over the pasta and toss carefully. Serve immediately.

Serves 4
kcal 287; KJ 1217; Protein 9 g; Fat 4 g;
CHO 57 g

variation _____

Deli Pasta with Chilled Chilli and Herb Dressing

Preparation time: 5 minutes, plus chilling
Cooking time: 12 minutes

- 300 g/10 oz dried angel hair
  spaghetti

DRESSING:

- 2 tablespoons Thai chilli
  dipping sauce
- 3 tablespoons light soy
  sauce
- 2 tablespoons chopped fresh
  coriander
- grated rind and juice of 1
  lime

1 Break the pasta into small pieces and cook, following step 1 of the main recipe.

2 Meanwhile, mix together the dressing ingredients in a small bowl and stir well to combine.

3 Drain the pasta and tip into a large bowl. Pour the dressing over the pasta, toss well and serve chilled.

Serves 4
kcal 272; KJ 1157; Protein 11 g; Fat 2 g;
CHO 58 g

Desserts and Baking

Looking for a sweet treat to round off a meal? For a special occasion, try the Cappuccino Pavlova; in the height of summer, the Mini Strawberry Shortcakes would fit the bill; whereas on a cold day, the Baked Plum Crumble would be a welcome warmer. And for a mid-morning break, what could be better than Moist Beetroot Cake with a cup of coffee?

Bite-Sized Cappuccino Meringues

Preparation time: 10–15 minutes
Cooking time: 20–25 minutes
Oven temperature: 180°C (350°F), Gas Mark 4

- 3 small egg whites
- 175 g/6 oz caster sugar
- 1 teaspoon strong black coffee or coffee and chicory essence
- 250 g/8 oz low-fat fromage frais
- strawberries, to serve
- cocoa powder, for dusting (optional)

1 Whisk the egg whites until they are stiff. Fold in 1 tablespoon of the sugar and then gradually whisk in the remainder. The meringue must be glossy and form peaks when spoonfuls are dropped back into the bowl. Fold in the coffee or coffee essence.

2 Drop spoonfuls of the meringue on to a baking sheet lined with baking paper. Cook in a preheated oven, 180°C (350°F), Gas Mark 4, for 20–25 minutes, or until the meringues are golden and crisp. Remove from the oven and cool for at least *10 minutes* before peeling off the paper. Repeat with the remaining meringue to make 24 in total.

3 Sandwich the meringues together in pairs with the fromage frais and serve immediately with strawberries and a dusting of cocoa powder, if liked.

Makes 12
kcal 73; KJ 313; Protein 2 g; Fat 0 g; CHO 17 g

variation _____

Cappuccino Pavlova

Preparation time: 10 minutes
Cooking time: 1 hour
Oven temperature: 120°C (250°F), Gas Mark ½

- ingredients as above
- 125 g/4 oz strawberries, hulled and chopped
- 125 g/4 oz fresh pineapple, cut into chunks

1 Make the meringue following step 1 of the main recipe. Spread the meringue mixture over a sheet of baking paper to form a circle measuring 20 cm/8 inches in diameter. Make a slight hollow in the centre of the meringue and cook in a preheated oven, 120°C (250°F), Gas Mark ½, for *1 hour*, or until the meringue is crisp. Remove from the oven and cool on the paper for about *10 minutes* before peeling off.

2 Stir the strawberries and pineapple chunks into the fromage frais and pile into the centre of the meringue. Dust with a little cocoa powder and serve.

Serves 4
kcal 243; KJ 1036; Protein 8 g; Fat 0 g;
CHO 56 g

Plum Sorbet

Preparation time: 5 minutes
Cooking time: 55 minutes, plus freezing
Oven temperature: 200°C (400°F), Gas Mark 6

- 750 g/1½ lb Victoria plums,
  halved and stoned
- 250 g/8 oz caster sugar
- 600 ml/1 pint water
- 1 cinnamon stick
- lemon peel strip

TO DECORATE:

- 1 plum, cut into 4 slices
- mint sprigs

1 Place the plums in a roasting tin and cook in a preheated oven, 200°C (400°F), Gas Mark 6, for *45 minutes*.

2 Meanwhile, put the sugar, water, cinnamon stick and lemon peel into a saucepan. Slowly dissolve the sugar over a low heat and then bring to the boil. Cook over a medium heat for *20 minutes*, or until the mixture is syrupy.

3 Transfer the cooked plums to the sugar syrup and cook for a further *10 minutes*. Remove the pan from the heat and discard the lemon peel and cinnamon stick.

4 Purée the fruit mixture in a blender or food processor, or rub through a sieve. Cool and freeze for *3 hours* until just frozen. Remove from the freezer and mash with a fork. Return to the freezer for a further *3 hours*.

5 Remove the sorbet from the freezer *10 minutes* before you are ready to serve. Decorate with plum slices and mint sprigs.

Serves 4
kcal 310; KJ 1322; Protein 1 g; Fat 0 g;
CHO 81 g

Three Fruit Compôte

Preparation time: 5 minutes, plus chilling
Cooking time: 10 minutes

- 2 ripe pears, peeled, cored and quartered
- 250 ml/8 fl oz freshly squeezed orange juice
- 50 ml/2 fl oz dark rum
- ½ cinnamon stick
- 175 g/6 oz seedless black grapes, halved
- ½ firm honeydew melon, peeled, deseeded and cut into large chunks
- ground cinnamon, to dust
- dessert biscuits, to serve

1 Put the pears, orange juice, rum and cinnamon stick into a large saucepan. Cover and simmer for *5 minutes*. Add the remaining fruit and simmer for a further *5 minutes*.

2 Remove from the heat and transfer to a bowl. Chill overnight and remove the cinnamon before serving. Decorate with a dusting of ground cinnamon, if liked. Serve with dessert biscuits.

Serves 4
kcal 144; KJ 611; Protein 2 g; Fat 0 g; CHO 29 g

Mini Strawberry Shortcakes

Preparation time: 20 minutes, plus chilling

- 8 low-fat digestive biscuits
- 4 teaspoons low-sugar
  strawberry jam
- 250 g/8 oz very low-fat
  cream cheese
- 2 teaspoons icing sugar
- 250 g/8 oz strawberries
- icing sugar, to decorate

1 Hull and slice the strawberries, reserving 4 for decoration. Fan the 4 reserved strawberries.

2 Spread a digestive biscuit with 1 teaspoon of the strawberry jam. Beat the cream cheese to soften and stir in the icing sugar, then spread one-quarter of it over the biscuit. Lay a few strawberry slices on top of the cream cheese, then top with a second biscuit. Lay a fanned strawberry on top and dust with icing sugar.

3 Repeat to make 3 more shortcakes. Chill for at least *1 hour* before serving.

Serves 4
kcal 187; KJ 789; Protein 7 g; Fat 5 g; CHO 29 g

Bara Brith

Preparation time: 10 minutes, plus soaking
Cooking time: 2 hours
Oven temperature: 150°C (300°F), Gas Mark 2

- 250 ml/8 fl oz strong cold tea
- 4 tablespoons marmalade
- 175 g/6 oz sultanas
- 200 g/7 oz golden granulated sugar
- 300 g/10 oz self-raising flour
- 2 eggs, beaten
- good pinch of mixed spice

1 Put the cold tea into a bowl with the marmalade and sultanas. Leave to soak for *1 hour*.

2 Stir in the remaining ingredients and mix well. Spoon the mixture into a greased 1 kg/2 lb loaf tin. Cook in a preheated oven, 150°C (300°F), Gas Mark 2, for *2 hours*, or until a skewer, when inserted, comes out clean.

Serves 8–10
kcal 408; KJ 1738; Protein 7 g; Fat 2 g;
CHO 96 g

Turkish Delight

Preparation time: 5 minutes
Cooking time: 30 minutes, plus chilling

- 25 g/1 oz gelatine
- 300 ml/½ pint water
- 500 g/1 lb granulated sugar
- ½ teaspoon citric acid
- 1 tablespoon rose water

- ¼ teaspoon red food colouring
- 50 g/2 oz icing sugar
- ½ teaspoon bicarbonate of soda

1 Sprinkle the gelatine into the water in a small bowl and set over a pan of simmering water. Allow to dissolve.

2 Put the granulated sugar and citric acid into a saucepan and add the dissolved gelatine. Simmer over a low heat for *10 minutes*. Remove from the heat and stir in the rose water and red food colouring. Cool before pouring into an oiled 20 cm/8 inch shallow square tin.

3 Chill overnight. Toss the icing sugar and bicarbonate of soda together. Cut the Turkish delight into diamonds and toss them in the sherbet mixture.

Makes 20 pieces
Per piece: kcal 113; KJ 480; Protein 1 g; Fat 0 g; CHO 29 g

Baked Braeburns with Lemon

Preparation time: 10 minutes
Cooking time: 45 minutes
Oven temperature: 180°C (350°F), Gas Mark 4

- 4 large Braeburn (or Cox or Granny Smith) apples
- 1 lemon, cut into 4 segments
- 50 g/2 oz light muscovado sugar
- 1 teaspoon cinnamon

1 Carefully remove the core from the middle of each apple. Using a small knife make the hole in the centre of each apple slightly larger. Put the lemon segments in a bowl and scatter the sugar and cinnamon over.

2 Once coated, push a lemon wedge into the centre of each apple. Arrange the apples in a small roasting tin lined with foil, then bake in a preheated oven, 180°C (350°F), Gas Mark 4, for *45 minutes*. Serve with low-fat fromage frais, if liked.

Serves 4
kcal 102; KJ 435; Protein 1 g; Fat 0 g; CHO 26 g

Baked Pineapple Rings with Cinnamon

Preparation time: 5 minutes
Cooking time: 20 minutes
Oven temperature: 200°C (400°F), Gas Mark 6

- 1 small pineapple, peeled
  and cored
- 50 g/2 oz dark muscovado
  sugar
- 1 teaspoon ground
  cinnamon
- pinch of mild chilli powder
- caster sugar, for dusting

1 Cut the pineapple into 1 cm/½ inch rings. Pat each ring dry on kitchen paper. Put the remaining ingredients into a large polythene bag. Toss well. Add a few pineapple rings to the bag. Toss well and then place the coated rings in a roasting tin. Repeat with the remaining rings.

2 Put on a baking tray lined with foil and dust with caster sugar. Cook in a preheated oven, 200°C (400°F), Gas Mark 6, for *20 minutes*. Serve with low-fat fromage frais, if liked.

Serves 4
kcal 100; KJ 430; Protein 1 g; Fat 0 g; CHO 26 g

variation
Caribbean Skewers

Preparation time: 15–20 minutes
Cooking time: 20 minutes

- 1 small pineapple, peeled,
  cored and cut into chunks
- 1 firm banana, cut into
  chunks
- 3 tablespoons runny honey
- 2 tablespoons lemon juice

1 Soak 8 wooden skewers in warm water for *10 minutes*. Drain. Thread the chunks of pineapple and banana on to the skewers. Mix together the runny honey and the lemon juice.

2 Arrange the skewers on a grill pan. Brush each with the honey marinade and grill under a medium heat for *20 minutes*, turning occasionally until the fruit has cooked.

Serves 4
kcal 140; KJ 600; Protein 1 g; Fat 0 g; CHO 36 g

Moist Beetroot Cake

Preparation time: 15 minutes
Cooking time: 45 minutes
Oven temperature: 180°C (350°F), Gas Mark 4

- 250 g/8 oz self-raising flour
- ½ teaspoon ground nutmeg
- ½ teaspoon ground mixed
  spice
- 150 g/5 oz light muscovado
  sugar
- ½ ripe banana, mashed
- 250 g/8 oz fresh cooked
  beetroot, peeled and finely
  grated

- 2 small eggs, beaten
- 125 ml/2 fl oz fat-free milk
- 250 g/8 oz fat-free fromage
  frais

1 Grease and line a 20 cm/8 inch shallow square cake tin. Sift the flour and spices into a large bowl. Stir in the sugar, banana and all but 25 g/1 oz of the beetroot.

2 Make a well in the centre and add the eggs and milk. Beat well, then pour the mixture into the prepared cake tin.

3 Cook the cake in a preheated oven, 180°C (350°F), Gas Mark 4, for *45 minutes*, or until a skewer inserted into the centre comes out clean. Leave to cool in the tin for *10 minutes*, then turn out on to a wire rack to cool.

4 Spread the fromage frais over the cake and scatter the remaining beetroot pieces over the top. Cut into 12 squares and serve.

Makes 12 squares
Per square: kcal 185; KJ 788; Protein 6 g;
Fat 2 g; CHO 40 g

variation _____

Sweet Parsnip Cake

Preparation time: 15 minutes
Cooking time: 1 hour
Oven temperature: 180°C (350°F), Gas Mark 4

1 Make up the cake mixture as above, replacing the beetroot and bananas with 250 g/8 oz raw grated parsnip and 125 ml/4 fl oz skimmed milk. Pour the mixture into the tin and cook as above for about *1 hour*, or until a skewer inserted into the centre comes out clean. Cool and cut into 12 squares.

Makes 12 squares
Per square: kcal 185; KJ 787; Protein 5 g;
Fat 2 g; CHO 40 g

Chewy Flapjack Squares

Preparation time: 10 minutes
Cooking time: 40 minutes
Oven temperature: 180°C (350°F), Gas Mark 4

- 75 g/3 oz low-fat spread
- 175 g/6 oz golden granulated
  sugar
- 100 g/4 oz golden syrup
- 5 tablespoons skimmed milk
- 375 g/12 oz rolled oats

- 500 g/1 lb peeled cooking
  apples, cored and sliced
- 25 g/1 oz caster sugar
- ¼ teaspoon ground cloves
- 2 tablespoons lemon juice

1 Melt the low-fat spread in a pan with the sugar, syrup and milk. Stir in the oats. Spoon two-thirds of the mixture into a greased 18 cm/7 inch shallow square tin and cook in a preheated oven, 180°C (350°F), Gas Mark 4, for *20 minutes*.

2 Meanwhile, place the apples in a saucepan with the caster sugar, ground cloves and lemon juice and cook until thick and pulpy. Spread the apple over the cooked oat base. Spread the remaining oat mixture over the top and cook for a further *20 minutes*. Allow to cool before cutting into 12 fingers.

Makes 12 fingers
**Per finger: kcal 255; KJ 1080; Protein 5 g;
Fat 5 g; CHO 50 g**

Baked Plum Crumble

Preparation time: 10 minutes
Cooking time: 35 minutes
Oven temperature: 200°C (400°F), Gas Mark 6

- 500 g/1 lb plums, halved and
  stoned
- 2 tablespoons runny honey
- 2.5 cm/1 inch piece of fresh
  root ginger, grated
- pinch of cinnamon
- grated rind and juice of 1
  orange

TOPPING:

- 125 g/4 oz sugar-free muesli
- 50 g/2 oz low-fat digestive
  biscuits, crushed
- 50 g/2 oz plain flour
- 25 g/1 oz low-fat spread

1 Arrange the plums in an ovenproof dish. Top with the honey, ginger, cinnamon and orange juice and rind.

2 Cook in a preheated oven, 200°C (400°F), Gas Mark 6, for *15 minutes*. Meanwhile, put all the remaining ingredients into a bowl and mix to form the crumb topping.

3 Remove the plums from the oven and scatter the crumble mixture over. Continue cooking for *20 minutes*. Serve with low-fat custard or a very low-fat fromage frais, if liked.

Serves 6
kcal 217; KJ 916; Protein 4 g; Fat 5 g; CHO 41 g

Special Photography:
Simon Smith
Home Economist:
Sally Mansfield
Jacket Photographer:
Simon Smith
Jacket Home Economist:
Sally Mansfield
Other Photography:
Reed Consumer Books Ltd./
Bryce Attwell/Jean Cazals/
Simon Smith/Roger Stowell